Internet
Scavenger Hunts
American History

Instant Reproducibles for 20 Exciting Internet Explorations That Enrich Learning and Get Kids Web-Savvy

by Michelle Robinette

SCHOLASTIC
PROFESSIONAL BOOKS

New York • Toronto • London • Auckland • Sydney • Mexico City
New Delhi • Hong Kong • Buenos Aires

Cover design by **Norma Ortiz**
Interior design by **Holly Grundon**
Illustrations by **Delana Bettoli**

Cover image: "The Underground Railroad" Web page reproduced courtesy of National Geographic Society.

ISBN 0-439-31665-0
Copyright © 2002 by Scholastic Inc.
All rights reserved.
Printed in the U.S.A.

2 3 4 5 6 7 8 9 10   40   08 07 06 05 04 03 02

Contents

Introduction 4

Native Americans 8

Early Explorers 12

Pilgrims 15

Colonial Life 18

American Revolution 21

A New Nation 24

Louisiana Purchase 27

Lewis & Clark 29

Oregon Trail 32

Slavery 35

Civil War 38

Gold Rush 40

Women's Suffrage 42

The Great Depression 44

World War I 46

World War II 48

Civil Rights Movement 50

Vietnam War 53

Space Exploration 55

American Pride 58

Answers 61

Introduction

In the last few years, the Internet has grown to become such an important resource for almost everyone that it's hard to imagine what life was like before it existed. As a teacher, you may use the Internet to search for lesson plans and activities, communicate with other teachers and classrooms from around the country, and get advice from professional developers.

Students are getting into the act, too. Just look at these facts about Internet usage in U.S. public schools from Quality Education Data (2001):

- 97 percent of America's public schools are connected to the Internet

- 84 percent of all public school classrooms are connected to the Internet

- 74 percent of students spend one hour or more per week hands-on at school with the Internet

- 96 percent of students who use the Internet weekly use it for research

Just because students spend a lot of time on the Internet, it doesn't mean that they can effectively conduct research on it. Just as it's necessary for students to learn library research skills, it's also important to teach them how to do research on the Internet. That's where *Internet Scavenger Hunts: American History* comes in.

Using This Book

Inside, you'll find more than 50 reproducible pages of Internet scavenger hunts on 20 American history topics that you teach. Scavenger hunts offer a quick and easy way to give your students practice in doing research on the Internet.

Some of the activity sheets require students to find basic facts, such as what foods were served during the first Thanksgiving, which side won some of the major battles in the Revolutionary War, and what job Sally Ride had as an astronaut. Other activities go beyond the facts and build students' critical-thinking skills — students write an advice column for pioneers planning to travel on the Oregon Trail, or design a poster to rally support and boost Americans' morale during World War II.

Use these self-guided scavenger hunts to introduce students to a new topic, supplement your lesson plan, or assign them as independent work.

Accessing the Web Sites

Ready to get students started on their Internet scavenger hunts? Send them to our Web site at:

http://www.scholastic.com/profbooks/easyinternet/index.htm

This address appears at the top of each reproducible activity page. When students reach this site, have them click on the book thumbnail of *Internet Scavenger Hunts: American History*. This will take them directly to a page that lists all the links for the activities. You may want to bookmark this site or add it to your favorites. To access the Web sites needed to complete each activity, have students click on the links under the activity name.

Even though we regularly update the links on our Web site, you may still want to check the links yourself before using them in your classroom. This way, you can make sure that the material on the site is appropriate for your students, and familiarize yourself with the content so you can help students as needed.

TIPS

for a

SUCCESSFUL HUNT

The activities in this book are designed so students can work independently, either individually or in small groups. To help students get the most out of their time online, share with them these helpful tips before they embark on their Internet scavenger hunts:

1. Read the activity sheet carefully before going to the computer. This way, students will know ahead of time what kind of information they need to find. You may want to go over the worksheet as a class to discuss any questions students may have.

2. Browse through the Web site for relevant information. Tell students that they don't have to read everything on the site. They can just skim through until they find the information they need. Have them refer back to their worksheets regularly so they know what to look for next.

3. Explore the various links on the page to get more information. On some Web sites, certain pictures or words within the text may be highlighted or underlined. Clicking on these links usually opens another page that gives more in-depth information. (Note: As much as possible, we've tried to avoid Web sites with advertisements. However, some very useful sites do have them. Caution students against clicking on any ads that may appear on a page.)

4. Use the commands Find or Find Again under the Edit toolbar to help search for a particular word on the Web page. For example, if students are looking for the definition of "imperialism," they could quickly look for the word on the Web page by using the command Find.

for the
ONE-COMPUTER CLASSROOM

You say you only have one computer in your classroom? With a few management tips, your class can still enjoy doing the activities in this book:

1. Hook up your computer to a video monitor or a projector so that the class can browse the Web together. Invite students to participate by taking turns clicking on the hyperlinks or reading the information.

2. You can save Web pages as viewable documents. Or, you can print out a Web site beforehand and hand out photocopies to students. Just make sure that you print out all the relevant pages and links that your students need to complete their activity pages.

3. If you have other computers in your classroom that aren't hooked up to the Internet, use an offline software such as Web Whacker to capture and download all the pages of a Web site.

4. Assign small groups of students to work together on the computer for about 15 to 20 minutes in rotation. Give the rest of the class other related activities to do while waiting their turn on the computer.

5. If students have access to the Internet at home, consider assigning the pages as homework. You can get them started on Step 1 and have them finish their work at home.

Enjoy!

Name: _____ Date: _____

GO TO: http://www.scholastic.com/profbooks/easyinternet/index.htm

Native Americans

The First Americans

Long before European explorers "discovered" America, other people had already settled on the land. Explore the links at the above Web site to learn more about these first Americans. Then compare the lives of early Native Americans and Americans today. Fill in the chart below.

	Early Native Americans	Modern-Day Americans
Food		
Clothing		
Housing		
Recreation		
Political Organization		

Name: _____ Date: _____

GO TO: http://www.scholastic.com/profbooks/easyinternet/index.htm

Native Americans

Iroquois of the Northeast

Some historians say that the Iroquois was the most important Native American group in American history. Find out more about this large tribe by clicking on the links at the above Web site. Then answer the questions below.

1. What name did the Iroquois
   Confederacy call themselves? _____

2. How many nations make up the Iroquois Confederacy? _____

3. What is wampum and how do the Iroquois use it? _____

   _____

4. What were the "Three Sisters"? _____

5. How did women contribute to life in the Iroquois camp? _____

   _____

6. What were the roles of the Iroquois men? _____

7. How long could the meat from one deer feed an Iroquois family? _____

8. After the depletion of land and game in the 19th century,
   how did the Iroquois people earn a living? _____

9. Which tribe of Iroquois is known for their iron-working skills? _____

10. What is the Great Law of Peace of the Iroquois people? _____

   _____

Internet Scavenger Hunts: American History   **9**

GO TO: http://www.scholastic.com/profbooks/easyinternet/index.htm

Native Americans

Cherokee of the Southeast

The Cherokee was one of the largest and most prosperous tribes that inhabited the southeast. Click on the links at the above Web site to learn about this group's history. Then solve this crossword puzzle.

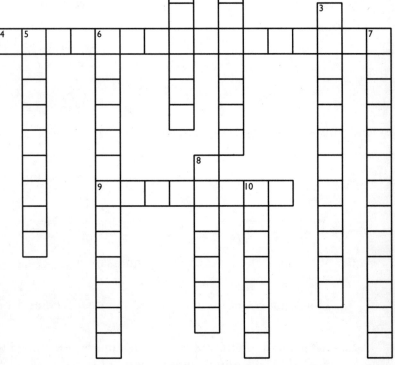

Across

4. Law passed by Congress in 1830 to move the Cherokee

9. Cherokee chief who fought against the removal of his people

Down

1. March of the Cherokee from their home to Oklahoma

2. The first Cherokee newspaper

3. Congressman who supported the Cherokee's fight against relocation

5. Cherokee's established capital in 1825

6. U.S. President who forced the Cherokee from their home

7. Name of the Cherokee alphabet

8. Side supported by the Cherokee during the American Revolution

10. Inventor of the Cherokee alphabet

Name: _____ Date: _____

GO TO: http://www.scholastic.com/profbooks/easyinternet/index.htm

Native Americans
Indians of the Great Plains

Old western movies often portray "Indians" as fierce, red-skinned warriors shooting at cowboys or Union soldiers. In fact, there were many conflicts between the "white man" and Plains Indians. But was one side always in the right? Click on the links at the above Web site to read about the various skirmishes between the two groups. Choose three significant events and write about them below. In each case, write who you think was in the wrong and why you think so.

	Event	What Happened?	Who was at fault?
1.			
2.			
3.			

GO TO: http://www.scholastic.com/profbooks/easyinternet/index.htm

Early Explorers

Leif Ericsson

Viking Leif Ericsson arrived in North America almost 500 years before Christopher Columbus. Click on the links at the above Web site to read an account of Ericsson's voyage to North America.
Then write a letter to the President of the United States requesting that Leif Ericsson be given the same recognition as Columbus. Be sure to include factual information to back up your claims.

Sincerely,

Name: _____ Date: _____

Early Explorers

Vespucci and Columbus

Amerigo Vespucci and Christopher Columbus were fellow explorers who had explored the "New World" extensively. However, a mapmaker of the time decided to name the newly discovered continents after Amerigo, labeling them North and South America. Click on the links at the above Web site to learn more about the two men. Then use the Venn diagram below to compare them.

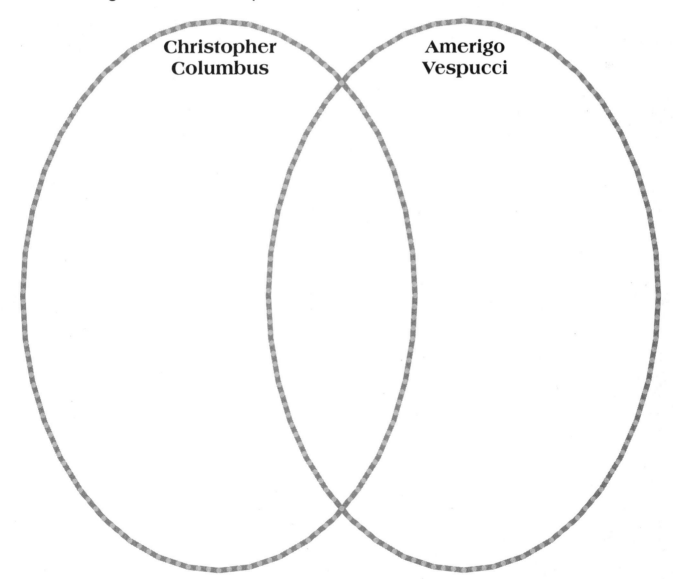

Christopher Columbus   Amerigo Vespucci

Name: _____ Date: _____

GO TO: http://www.scholastic.com/profbooks/easyinternet/index.htm

Early Explorers

Columbus: The Myth Behind the Man

We've all heard the rhyme, "In 1492, Columbus sailed the ocean blue." But what else do we know about Christopher Columbus? How much of what we've been told is really true? Visit the links at the above Web site to separate truth from fiction. Record five facts and five myths about Columbus in the chart below.

	Facts	Myths
1.		
2.		
3.		
4.		
5.		

GO TO: http://www.scholastic.com/profbooks/easyinternet/index.htm

Pilgrims

Coming to America

The Pilgrims who came to America left England yearning for religious freedom. Read about their journey on the *Mayflower* by clicking on the links at the above Web site. Then, pretend that you are a Pilgrim. Write a journal entry describing life on the *Mayflower*, plus your hopes, fears, and plans for your new home. Use facts from the Web sites to make your entry as realistic as possible.

Trivia Tracker

What was the name of the child born during the crossing of the *Mayflower*?

_____

September 1620

Dear Diary,

_____

_____

_____

_____

_____

_____

_____

_____

_____

Name: _____ Date: _____

GO TO: http://www.scholastic.com/profbooks/easyinternet/index.htm

Pilgrims

The First Thanksgiving

When we think of the first Thanksgiving, we probably envision Pilgrims and Indians seated around a table enjoying a delicious feast. Find out what the event was actually like by visiting the links at the above Web site. Then answer the questions below.

1. WHY was the feast held? _____

2. WHO joined the feast? _____

_____

3. WHAT foods were served? _____

_____

4. WHEN was it held? _____

5. WHERE was it held? _____

6. Other facts about the first Thanksgiving _____

_____

_____

_____

Name: _____   Date: _____

GO TO: http://www.scholastic.com/profbooks/easyinternet/index.htm

Pilgrims

Life at Plymouth

The Pilgrims were eager to establish a new home at Plymouth—but the Wampanoag Indians were already living there. Explore the links at the above Web site to learn more about the daily life of the Pilgrims and the Indians at Plymouth. Then complete the activities below.

1. Who was the infamous assistant to Governor Bradford?

_____

2. Who was the Wampanoag Indian who served as an interpreter between the Pilgrims and the Indians?

_____

3. What diseases did the Pilgrims bring with them to Plymouth?

_____

Trivia Tracker

When did the *Mayflower* return home to England?

_____

Compare the lifestyles of Pilgrims and Wampanoag Indians below.

	Pilgrims	Wampanoag
Clothing		
Food		
Home		
Education		
Games		

Name: _____ Date: _____

GO TO: http://www.scholastic.com/profbooks/easyinternet/index.htm

Colonial Life

Establishing the Colonies

Life in the newly established American colonies was full of excitement and adventure. Browse the links at the above Web site, then figure out which of the following statements are true or false. Rewrite the false statements to make them true.

Trivia Tracker

Which minister did Puritan leaders want to send back to England? What colony did he later establish?

_____

_____

True or False?

_____ 1. The Quakers settled in Oregon in 1682.

_____ 2. Georgia was settled as a colony in 1733.

_____ 3. The colony of Jamestown was named after St. James.

_____ 4. The colony of St. Mary's in Maryland later changed its name to Baltimore.

_____ 5. William Penn was one of the Puritan leaders.

_____ 6. South Carolina was settled in 1670.

_____ 7. The Pilgrims started out from England on a ship called the *Speedwell*.

_____ 8. The Puritans first settled in Connecticut before moving to Massachusetts.

_____ 9. New Netherlands became New York in 1623.

_____ 10. The Dutch hired English captain Henry Hudson to look for a westward passage to the Indies.

Name: _____ Date: _____

Colonial Life

The First Permanent Colony

Jamestown, Virginia, was the first permanent English colony in America. Click on the links at the above Web site to learn more about the people of Jamestown. Pretend that you're one of the first colonists in Jamestown and write a letter to a friend in England. Use information found in the Web sites to tell your friend about your new life.

Name: _____   Date: _____

Colonial Life

The Boston Tea Party

The Boston Tea Party was no party at all, but rather an act of protest against England. Learn about the events that led to the Boston Tea Party and the actual event itself by browsing through the links at the above Web site. Then create a comic strip below that tells about the Boston Tea Party, including events leading up to and following the protest.

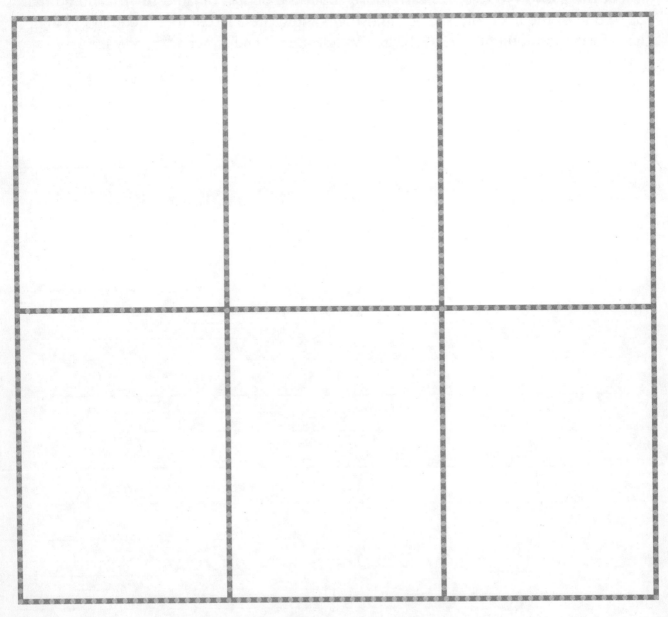

Name: _____ Date: _____

GO TO: http://www.scholastic.com/profbooks/easyinternet/index.htm

American Revolution

Revolutionary Journal

The colonists in America were determined to gain their freedom from the overbearing English government. Visit the links at the above Web site to gain a better understanding of the Revolutionary War. Pretend you're a student living in a newly established colony. Record events happening around you during the American Revolution over several years.

1765 _____
_____
_____
_____

1768 _____
_____
_____
_____

1770 _____
_____
_____
_____

1776 _____
_____
_____
_____

Name: _____   Date: _____

GO TO: http://www.scholastic.com/profbooks/easyinternet/index.htm

American Revolution

Battles of the Revolution

Many battles were fought during the Revolutionary War—not all brought victory to the colonists. Click on the links at the above Web site to learn about some of these famous battles.

Trivia Tracker

What was General Israel Putnam's infamous quote?

_____

_____

Battles of Lexington and Concord

When? _____

Where? _____

Key Figures? _____

_____

Outcome? _____

_____

Battle of Saratoga

When? _____

Where? _____

Key Figures? _____

_____

Outcome? _____

_____

Battle of Bunker Hill

When? _____

Where? _____

Key Figures? _____

_____

Outcome? _____

_____

Battle of Trenton

When? _____

Where? _____

Key Figures? _____

_____

Outcome? _____

_____

Name: _____ Date: _____

American Revolution
People of the Revolution

During the American Revolution, some people stood out more than others. Check out the links at the above Web site to familiarize yourself with some of the significant players of the war. Write a short biographical sketch of each person below, including his or her role in the war.

Paul Revere _____

_____

_____

Ethan Allen _____

_____

_____

Nathan Hale _____

_____

_____

Deborah Sampson _____

_____

_____

Name: _____   Date: _____

GO TO: http://www.scholastic.com/profbooks/easyinternet/index.htm

A New Nation

Who Were Our Founding Fathers?

On May 14, 1787, a group of men from the original
colonies (except Rhode Island) attended the Constitutional
Convention in Philadelphia to discuss the creation of the
U.S. Constitution. Read about the people who attended the
Convention on the links at the above Web site. Choose
five delegates and complete their mini-biographies below.

Trivia Tracker

How many states
are represented in
the signature area of
the Constitution?

_____

1.
Name _____
Home State _____
Outstanding Attribute _____

2.
Name _____
Home State _____
Outstanding Attribute _____

3.
Name _____
Home State _____
Outstanding Attribute _____

4.
Name _____
Home State _____
Outstanding Attribute _____

5.
Name _____
Home State _____
Outstanding Attribute _____

Name: _____ Date: _____

GO TO: http://www.scholastic.com/profbooks/easyinternet/index.htm

A New Nation
The Declaration of Independence

Considered one of our country's most important documents, the Declaration of Independence is a list of complaints the United States had against the King of England. Read the Declaration of Independence by clicking on the links at the above Web site. Then pick five grievances and rewrite them in easy-to-understand words below.

> **Trivia Tracker**
>
> How old was Thomas Jefferson when he drafted the Declaration of Independence?
>
> _____

Reason #1 _____

_____

Reason #2 _____

_____

Reason #3 _____

_____

Reason #4 _____

_____

Reason #5 _____

_____

GO TO: http://www.scholastic.com/profbooks/easyinternet/index.htm

A New Nation
The First President

George Washington, the first president of the United States, will always be known as the father of our country. Research his life by exploring the links at the above Web site. Then complete the mini-biography of George Washington below.

Birth: _____

Parents: _____

Wife: _____

Number of Children: _____

Role in Revolutionary War: _____

Political Affiliation: _____

Year Elected President: _____

Vice President: _____

Year Left Office: _____

Death: _____

Trivia Tracker

What was the original name given to the home we now call Mount Vernon?

_____

Name: _____ Date: _____

GO TO: http://www.scholastic.com/profbooks/easyinternet/index.htm

Louisiana Purchase

The Greatest Real Estate Deal in History

In 1803, as president, Thomas Jefferson bought a large tract of land that nearly doubled the size of the United States. Click on the links at the above Web site to read about the Louisiana Purchase and how it changed our nation forever. Then answer the questions below.

1. What country previously owned the land involved in the Louisiana Purchase? _____

2. Who was the American minister who tried to convince Napoleon to sell this land? _____

3. How much did the United States pay for this vast amount of land? _____

4. About how much did the United States pay per acre for the Louisiana Territory? _____

5. How many states were created from the land bought through the Louisiana Purchase? _____

6. Look at this map of the United States. Shade in each state that was added to the United States through the Louisiana Purchase.

Name: _____ Date: _____

GO TO: http://www.scholastic.com/profbooks/easyinternet/index.htm

Louisiana Purchase

What If It Had Never Happened?

What might our country be like today if President Jefferson hadn't made the Louisiana Purchase? Click on the links at the above Web site. Then list 10 things that would be different about our country if the Louisiana Purchase had never occurred. (Think about the resources that land provides, the people, travel, communication, business, and more.)

Trivia Tracker

Who was Pierre Clement de Laussat and what was his role in the Louisiana Purchase?

_____

_____

1.	
2.	
3.	
4.	
5.	
6.	
7.	
8.	
9.	
10.	

Name: _____ Date: _____

GO TO: http://www.scholastic.com/profbooks/easyinternet/index.htm

Lewis & Clark

Getting to Know Lewis & Clark

In 1804, Meriwether Lewis and William Clark led an expedition to survey the new Louisiana territory. Write what you know about the Lewis and Clark expedition in the first column below. In the second column, write what you want to know about it. Click on the links at the above Web site and fill in the third column with new information you've learned.

What I Know	What I Want to Know	What I Learned

Name: _____ Date: _____

GO TO: http://www.scholastic.com/profbooks/easyinternet/index.htm

Lewis & Clark

The Men Behind the Expedition

Meriwether Lewis and William Clark became famous for bravely leading an expedition into unknown territory. But what else do we know about these two men? Why were they chosen to lead the expedition? After visiting the links at the above Web site, jot down 10 interesting facts about each explorer in the spaces below.

	Meriwether Lewis	William Clark
1.		
2.		
3.		
4.		
5.		
6.		
7.		
8.		
9.		
10.		

Name: _____   Date: _____

GO TO: http://www.scholastic.com/profbooks/easyinternet/index.htm

Lewis & Clark

The Tale of Sacagawea

Sacagawea, a Shoshone Indian, was the only woman to accompany the Lewis and Clark expedition. Her knowledge of the land and the people proved invaluable to the expedition. Explore the links at the above Web site to find out more about Sacagawea. Then answer the following questions.

1. What party of Indians kidnapped
   Sacagawea when she was a young girl? _____

2. What role did Sacagawea's father play in their Shoshone village? _____

3. To whom was Sacagawea married? _____

4. In what business was Sacagawea's husband involved? _____

5. Name two ways Sacagawea was helpful
   during the Lewis and Clark expedition. _____

   _____

6. What life-changing event happened
   to Sacagawea during the expedition? _____

7. Who was the leader of the group of
   Shoshones the expedition encountered? _____

8. What did Sacagawea receive upon the completion of the journey? _____

9. Sacagawea died soon after giving birth to a
   second child. What happened to her children? _____

10. What nickname did Clark give Sacagawea's son? _____

Name: _____   Date: _____

GO TO: http://www.scholastic.com/profbooks/easyinternet/index.htm

Oregon Trail

Dear Pappy Pioneer

The Oregon Trail was a major route for early immigrants moving to the West. More than 350,000 people traveled the 2,170-mile route westward between 1841 and 1867. Read about the people who traveled the Oregon Trail by clicking on the links at the above Web site. Imagine that you're an advice columnist for pioneers planning to move west. How would you answer these letters?

Dear Pappy Pioneer,

We live in Pennsylvania and we're yearning to follow that trail west. My wife wants to pack everything including the kitchen sink. What do we really need to bring?

Sincerely,
Packing in Pennsylvania

Dear Packing in Pennsylvania,

_____

_____

_____

_____

_____

_____

Sincerely,
Pappy Pioneer

Dear Pappy Pioneer,

I can't decide on which animals to use to pull our wagon: horses, mules, or oxen. Which do you think would get us all the way west?

Yours truly,
Beast of Burden

Dear Beast of Burden,

_____

_____

_____

_____

_____

_____

_____

Sincerely,
Pappy Pioneer

Name: _____ Date: _____

GO TO: http://www.scholastic.com/profbooks/easyinternet/index.htm

Oregon Trail

Landmarks by the Trail

Travelers on the trail encountered new and exciting sights along the way. Visit the links at the above Web site to learn more about points of interest the pioneers encountered. Write at least three sentences to describe each of the landmarks below.

Above Spring _____

_____

_____

Chimney Rock _____

_____

_____

South Pass _____

_____

_____

Three Island Crossing _____

_____

_____

Oregon City _____

_____

_____

Name: _____   Date: _____

GO TO: http://www.scholastic.com/profbooks/easyinternet/index.htm

Oregon Trail

Getting Ready to Leave

Take a trip back in time and pretend that you and your family are getting ready to move westward. Click on the links at the above Web site to assist you with your preparations.

Trivia Tracker

How much did it cost to buy 400 pounds of bacon, 6 pounds of pepper, and 2 frying pans back then?

_____

1. Why is your family moving west?

_____

_____

_____

2. How much money do you plan to carry? _____

3. How do you plan on spending your money? Make a list of things you plan to buy.

_____

_____

_____

_____

4. On another sheet of paper, sketch the trail route your family will follow. Mark the stops you plan to make on the way.

List the items you plan to carry:	
1.	
2.	
3.	
4.	
5.	
6.	
7.	
8.	
9.	
10.	

Name: _____ Date: _____

Slavery

The Life of a Slave

When the colonies were first established in America, Africans were brought over and sold to work as slaves in large plantations in the South. Click on the links at the above Web site to get a glimpse of what life was like on a southern plantation in the 1800s. Pretend you're a newspaper reporter from the North, sent to interview slaves in the South. Think of five questions you would like to ask and list them. Then think about how a slave might answer your questions and write the answers below.

Questions

1.

2.

3.

4.

5.

Answers

1.

2.

3.

4.

5.

Name: _____ Date: _____

GO TO: http://www.scholastic.com/profbooks/easyinternet/index.htm

Slavery

Journey to Freedom

The Underground Railroad was a series of trails, hideouts, and safe havens that slaves followed to freedom in the northern states. Click on the links at the above Web site to find out what it was like to travel the Underground Railroad. Then, imagine yourself on this journey. Write your thoughts in the journal entries below as you "travel" toward freedom.

Journal Entry #1 *(The First Days)*

_____

_____

_____

_____

Journal Entry #2 *(My Feelings as I Travel)*

_____

_____

_____

_____

Journal Entry #3 *(How It Feels to be Free)*

_____

_____

_____

_____

Name: _____ Date: _____

GO TO: http://www.scholastic.com/profbooks/easyinternet/index.htm

Slavery

The Moses of Her People

An escaped slave herself, Harriet Tubman risked her own safety many times to lead other slaves to freedom. She was called Moses by African-Americans. Visit the links at the above Web site to learn more about her. Using information you've found, write facts in each box that tell about Tubman's life.

Trivia Tracker

What price was offered for the capture of Harriet Tubman?

_____

Birth

Harriet Tubman

Adult Life

Childhood

Teen Years

Name: _____ Date: _____

GO TO: http://www.scholastic.com/profbooks/easyinternet/index.htm

Civil War

North and South

Even during colonial times, the differences between the northern and southern states were always apparent. These differences in geography, economics, and way of life eventually led to the War Between the States. Click on the links at the above Web site to gain a better understanding of the reasons behind the Civil War. Then compare the North and South using the Venn diagram below.

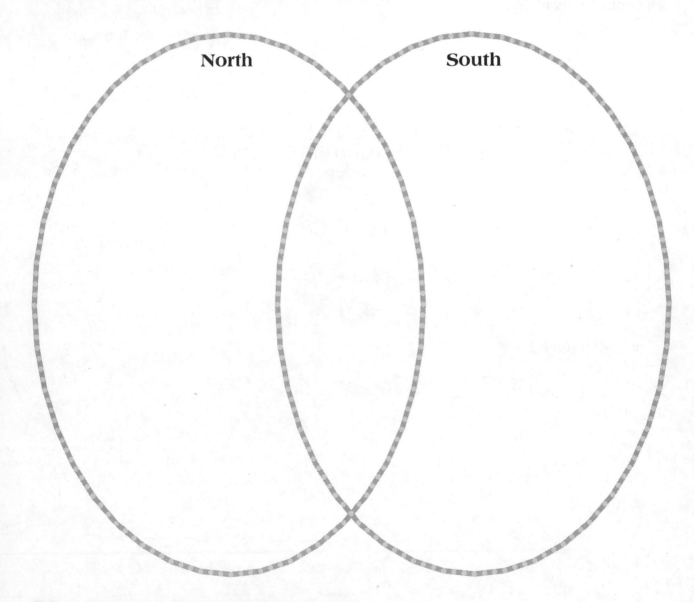

North   South

Name: _____ Date: _____

GO TO: http://www.scholastic.com/profbooks/easyinternet/index.htm

Civil War

Five Years of War

The Civil War started in April 1861 and ended in April 1865. Explore the links at the above Web site and list significant events that occurred during each of the years below. Then turn your lists into a classroom timeline. Add maps and illustrations to your final product!

1861

1. _____
2. _____
3. _____
4. _____
5. _____

1862

1. _____
2. _____
3. _____
4. _____
5. _____

1863

1. _____
2. _____
3. _____
4. _____
5. _____

1864

1. _____
2. _____
3. _____
4. _____
5. _____

1865

1. _____
2. _____
3. _____
4. _____
5. _____

Trivia Tracker

Who was Rose O'Neal Greenhow and what is she best known for during the Civil War?

_____

_____

Name: _____   Date: _____

Gold Rush

Golden Milestones

The California Gold Rush was the largest voluntary migration in the history of the United States. Thousands of Americans flocked to California hoping to make their fortunes. Visit the links at the above Web site to learn more about the Gold Rush. Fill in the timeline below with relevant facts.

Jan. 24, 1848 _____

Feb. 2, 1848 _____

March 9, 1848 _____

May 15, 1848 _____

Dec. 5, 1848 _____

April 11, 1849 _____

Sept. 9, 1850 _____

1854 _____

GO TO: http://www.scholastic.com/profbooks/easyinternet/index.htm

Gold Rush

What If?

The California Gold Rush was an exciting time for our new and growing country. Click on the links at the above Web site and read all the interesting information about the Gold Rush. Keep in mind what you've learned as you answer the "what if" questions below.

Trivia Tracker

Why did some miners pay as much as $100 for a drink of water?

_____

1. What if James Marshall had never discovered gold in the California territory?

   _____

   _____

   _____

2. What if the westward land that we now call California had never been added to the United States? What impact would this have on our country today?

   _____

   _____

   _____

3. What if you had been a settler in the early days? Would you have followed the trail to the California gold? Why?

   _____

   _____

   _____

Name: _____ Date: _____

GO TO: http://www.scholastic.com/profbooks/easyinternet/index.htm

Women's Suffrage

Women Fighters

The 15th Amendment to the Constitution guarantees every man in the United States—regardless of race or religion—the right to vote. Women, however, were completely left out. Around the 1800s, many women, called *suffragists*, fought for women's right to vote. Visit the links at the above Web site to learn about the women who fought long and hard for voting rights. Then write a mini-biography about each suffragist below.

Susan B. Anthony _____

_____

Elizabeth Cady Stanton _____

_____

Lucretia Coffin Mott _____

_____

Carrie Chapman Catt _____

_____

Sojourner Truth _____

_____

Amelia Bloomer _____

_____

Name: _____   Date: _____

Women's Suffrage

The 19ᵗʰ Amendment

The 19th Amendment to the Constitution, which guarantees all women the right to vote, was passed in 1920. Go to links at the above Web site to learn more about the 19th amendment. Then answer the questions below.

1. When was the 19th amendment first introduced in Congress? _____

2. On what date was the 19th amendment finally ratified? _____

3. What tactics did suffragists use in order to demonstrate
   the need for the ratification of the amendment? _____

   _____

4. How many states were required to ratify the amendment? _____

5. What important role did the state of Tennessee
   play in the ratification of the 19th amendment? _____

6. Who certified the 19th amendment? _____

7. Did many of the early suffrage supporters
   live to see the passing of the 19th amendment? _____

Children's Suffrage?

A growing number of people believe that citizens of any age should be allowed to vote. Click on the links at the above Web site to read more about children's suffrage, then voice your own opinion. Should children have the right to vote? Why or why not?

_____

_____

Name: _____ Date: _____

GO TO: http://www.scholastic.com/profbooks/easyinternet/index.htm

The Great Depression

The Lean Years

In late 1929, the United States economy started to slump faster than it ever had before. The result: Banks and businesses closed and many people lost their jobs and went hungry. Learn more about the Great Depression by clicking on the links at the above Web site. Then answer the questions below.

1. Name two other countries that were affected by the Great Depression.

    _____

2. Who was the president of the United States when the Great Depression began?

    _____

3. Compare unemployment in 1920 to 1933.

    _____

4. What does the term "rugged individualism" mean?

    _____

5. What were Hoovervilles?

    _____

6. What happened to the banks as people began to withdraw their money?

    _____

7. What were the three R's President Franklin D. Roosevelt wanted to offer the people of the United States?

    _____

8. Why did some of the wealthy people dislike President Roosevelt?

    _____

Name: _____ Date: _____

GO TO: http://www.scholastic.com/profbooks/easyinternet/index.htm

The Great Depression

How Much Does It Cost?

The prices of items and services have changed quite a bit since the days of the Great Depression. Look at the chart below and guess how much the items cost back then and today. Then click on the links at the above Web site to find the actual prices and fill in the chart below.

Product	Price Then		Price Now	
	Guess	Actual	Guess	Actual
Men's Overcoat				
Men's Wool Sweater				
Suede Bag				
Women's Sweater				
Women's Bathrobe				
Women's Overcoat				
Mechanical Toys				
Doll				
Lamp				
Electric Washing Machine				
Gas Stove				
Wages for a Cook				
Wages for a Doctor				

Name: _____   Date: _____

GO TO: http://www.scholastic.com/profbooks/easyinternet/index.htm

World War I

The Great War

World War I was sparked when an assassin shot the Archduke Franz Ferdinand of Austria-Hungary. Soon, several countries including the United States joined in the Great War. Check out the links at the above Web site to read more about World War I. Complete the table below by listing when each country got involved and why.

Trivia Tracker

What was the Red Baron's real name?

_____

Country	Date of First Involvement	Reason
Austria-Hungary		
Germany		
France		
Belgium		
Great Britain		
United States		
Russia		

Name: _____ Date: _____

GO TO: http://www.scholastic.com/profbooks/easyinternet/index.htm

World War I

The Causes of War

Some experts agree that World War I could have been avoided if it hadn't been for imperialism, militarism, nationalism, and alliances. Visit the links at the above Web site to gain a better understanding of each of these terms. Then write a brief explanation of each one in the spaces below.

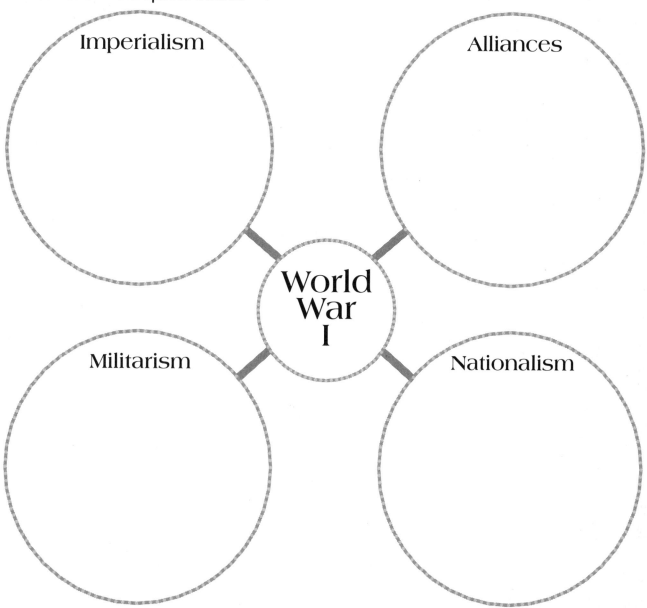

Name: _____   Date: _____

GO TO: http://www.scholastic.com/profbooks/easyinternet/index.htm

World War II

Posters of Persuasion

World War II had been raging for two years before the United States became involved. As battles were being fought on foreign ground, the U.S. government published war posters back home to boost the morale of Americans and gain their confidence in the war effort. Click on the links at the above Web site to view the posters. Then, create your own war slogan and design a poster to go with it.

Trivia Tracker

Who was George S. Patton, Jr. and what role did he play in World War II?

_____

_____

_____

Slogan

Name: _____   Date: _____

Word War II

D-Day

In the early hours of June 6, 1944, Allied soldiers crept up the beach of Normandy, France, and began a bloody attack that ultimately led to the downfall of Hitler's Nazi Germany. Click on the links at the above Web site to read more about D-Day and its outcome. Then answer the questions below.

Trivia Tracker

Who was Benito Mussolini? What was his involvement in World War II?

_____

_____

1. Describe the decoy the Allies created prior to the invasion. _____
   _____

2. What was the "Atlantic Wall"? _____

3. What was the code name for the D-Day invasion? _____

4. What is a B-17? _____

5. Why did so many Allied bombers miss their targets? _____

6. How many months after D-Day did Germany surrender? _____

7. What is a DUKW? _____

8. How many Allied soldiers were killed by the end of the day? _____

9. Approximately how many Allied ships approached the beach that day? _____

10. On what day was the invasion originally scheduled? _____

    Why didn't it occur on that day? _____

Name: _____ Date: _____

GO TO: http://www.scholastic.com/profbooks/easyinternet/index.htm

Civil Rights Movement

The Woman Who Refused to Stand

Rosa Parks, a seamstress in Montgomery, Alabama, is known as the "Mother of the Civil Rights Movement." Find out why by clicking on the links at the above Web site. Then write key events that happened in Rosa Park's life and the Civil Rights Movement in the timeline below.

Trivia Tracker

What had the same bus driver that had Rosa Parks arrested asked her to do 12 years earlier?

_____

December 1, 1955 _____

_____

December 2, 1955 _____

_____

December 5, 1955 _____

_____

November 13, 1956 _____

_____

November 14, 1956 _____

_____

Name: _____ Date: _____

Civil Rights Movement

Little Rock Nine

In 1957, Central High School in Little Rock, Arkansas, was forced to welcome its first African-American students. Amid enraged protesters, the Little Rock Nine (as the students were called) were escorted by the Army into the school on September 25. Visit the links at the above Web site to gain a better understanding of this historic event. Imagine that you are one of the Little Rock Nine. Write a journal entry below sharing your feelings about the first day of school and what you think the next day might bring. Use facts to help make your entry realistic.

_____

_____

_____

_____

_____

_____

_____

_____

_____

GO TO: http://www.scholastic.com/profbooks/easyinternet/index.htm

Civil Rights Movement

King of Civil Rights

A Baptist minister in Alabama, Dr. Martin Luther King, Jr., was the charismatic leader of the Civil Rights Movement. He believed in equal rights for everyone and spread his message of nonviolence. Explore the links at the above Web site, then jot down 10 interesting facts about the late Dr. King.

1.	
2.	
3.	
4.	
5.	
6.	
7.	
8.	
9.	
10.	

Name: _____ Date: _____

GO TO: http://www.scholastic.com/profbooks/easyinternet/index.htm

Vietnam War

War Against Communism

The Vietnam War was one of the costliest and deadliest wars the United States has ever fought in. Our government was trying to help non-Communist South Vietnam fend off Communist North Vietnam. Research the links at the above Web site to learn more about this war. Then answer the questions below.

Trivia Tracker

How many engraved granite panels make up the Vietnam Veterans Memorial Wall?

_____

1. How many lives were lost during the Vietnam War? _____

2. What was the average age of a soldier in Vietnam? _____

3. Which United States President decided that America would join the war and fight in "cold blood"? _____

4. Did soldiers serve the length of the war or tours of duty? _____

5. When did the first U.S. military group arrive in Vietnam? _____

6. Which president pulled the first group of troops out of South Vietnam? _____

7. How many servicemen are still unaccounted for? _____

8. What was the age of the oldest soldier killed in Vietnam? _____

Name: _____ Date: _____

GO TO: http://www.scholastic.com/profbooks/easyinternet/index.htm

Vietnam War

Timeline of Events

The Vietnam War was a complicated time in our
country's history. Click on the links at the above
Web site to read chronicles of the war. Then use the
chart below to record at least 10 years and events
you feel were significant during the Vietnam conflict.

Trivia Tracker

Who was
Ho Chi Minh?

_____

	Year	Important Event
1.		
2.		
3.		
4.		
5.		
6.		
7.		
8.		
9.		
10.		

Name: _____ Date: _____

GO TO: http://www.scholastic.com/profbooks/easyinternet/index.htm

Space Exploration

The Right Stuff

Imagine what it would be like to blast off in a rocket and float out in space. It's a job many would love to have. The National Aeronautics and Space Administration (NASA) receives thousands of applications every year, but picks less than 100 new applicants for astronaut training. Click on the links at the above Web site to learn more about what it takes to be an astronaut. Using information from the sites, write a help-wanted ad for astronauts below.

Trivia Tracker

Once chosen for the training program, where do astronauts go for their training?

_____

Help Wanted: Astronaut

_____

_____

_____

_____

_____

_____

_____

_____

Name: _____   Date: _____

GO TO: http://www.scholastic.com/profbooks/easyinternet/index.htm

Space Exploration

Ride, Sally Ride!

Sally Ride had just completed her doctorate degree in physics when she saw an ad in the local paper—NASA was looking for astronaut applicants and, this time, they were considering women as well. Sally Ride later became the first American woman in space. Visit the links at the above Web site. Pretend that you are Sally Ride on an interview. Answer the questions below.

1. When and where were you born? _____

2. What sport did you enjoy when you were young? _____

3. Where did you go to college? _____

4. What was the nickname given to your class at NASA? _____

5. What was so special about June 18, 1983? _____

6. What was your job or special area while with the astronaut corps? _____

7. How many days did you stay in orbit on your first mission? _____

8. What did President Reagan ask you to do? _____

9. How did Commander Crippen respond to people when they accused him of sending you to space because you were a woman? _____

    _____

10. What are you doing now? _____

Name: _____ Date: _____

GO TO: http://www.scholastic.com/profbooks/easyinternet/index.htm

Space Exploration

What's in Store for Space?

The U.S. space program has grown rapidly since it began in the 1950s. What does the future hold for space research? Check out the links at the above Web site. Then use the information you gather to form your own opinions about the future of our space program.

1. What new discoveries or programs do you think NASA will have made or developed by the year 2010? _____

_____

2. Do you think regular (non-astronaut) citizens will ever be allowed to travel on a NASA flight? Why or why not? _____

_____

3. Do you think there will ever be a permanent space station on the moon? Why or why not? _____

_____

4. If you could become part of NASA's program, what would you like your area of expertise to be? _____

_____

Name: _____ Date: _____

GO TO: http://www.scholastic.com/profbooks/easyinternet/index.htm

American Pride

Our Government

Our government is divided into three branches that work together to run the country. A system of checks and balances ensures that no branch exerts more power than the others. Learn more about how our government works by visiting the links at the above Web site. Use information you find to define the following terms:

Trivia Tracker

What is an electorate?

_____

_____

Amendment

_____

_____

Executive Branch

_____

_____

Checks and Balance

_____

_____

Judicial Branch

_____

_____

Constitutional

_____

_____

Legislative Branch

_____

_____

Electoral College

_____

_____

Republic

_____

_____

Name: _____ Date: _____

GO TO: http://www.scholastic.com/profbooks/easyinternet/index.htm

American Pride

Our Flag

Our flag symbolizes democracy, freedom, and other ideals of the United States. Over the years, our flag's design has changed, representing the growth of our nation. Explore the links at the above Web site to see how our flag has changed throughout history. Draw the United States flag as it appeared in the years below.

1777

1837

1863

1959

Name: _____ Date: _____

GO TO: http://www.scholastic.com/profbooks/easyinternet/index.htm

American Pride

The Star-Spangled Banner

As he watched Americans bravely defend Fort McHenry against British forces, poet-lawyer Francis Scott Key was inspired to write the poem that later became our National Anthem. Explore the Web sites to learn more about "The Star-Spangled Banner." Answer the following questions then pretend you're a reporter. Write a complete account of the events surrounding the creation of our National Anthem at the back of this page.

1. Who was Francis Scott Key?_____

2. Where was he when he was inspired to write the poem? _____

3. Why was Key in this location? _____
_____

4. Did he also write the music for the poem? _____

5. What did Key do after writing the anthem? _____
_____

6. What national monument features a tribute to Key? _____

7. When did the poem become the official National Anthem of the United States?_____

Answers

NATIVE AMERICANS

The First Americans (p. 8)
Answers may vary.

Iroquois of the Northeast (p. 9)
1. Haudenosaunee
2. 6
3. Shells or shell beads arranged in certain designs on a belt that represent significant events. Wampum was used as a memory aid to remember history, traditions, and rituals.
4. Corn, beans, squash
5. Headed the clan and led political life
6. Warrior and hunter
7. One week
8. Basketry, embroidery, beadwork
9. Mohawks
10. Iroquois shall not kill each other

Cherokee of the Southeast (p. 10)

```
          T
          R
          A
          I
          L
          O        P                   D
          F        H                   A
          T        E                   V
I N D I A N R E M O V A L A C T
E       N          N                 Y
W       D          I                 C
E       R          X                 R   W
C       E              B             O   A
H       W      J O H N R O S S       C   L
O       J          I     E           K   K
T       A          T     Q           E   I
A       C          I     U           T   N
        K          S     O           T   G
        S          H     Y               L
        O                A               E
        N                                A
                                         V
                                         E
                                         S
```

Indians of the Great Plains (p. 11)
Answers may vary.

EARLY EXPLORERS

Leif Ericsson (p. 12)
Answers may vary.

Vespucci and Columbus (p. 13)
Answers may vary.

Columbus: The Myth Behind the Man (p. 14)
Answers may vary.

PILGRIMS

Coming to America (p. 15)
Answers may vary.
Trivia Tracker: Oceanus

The First Thanksgiving (p. 16)
1. The Pilgrims were celebrating the fall harvest.
2. Answers may vary. There were more than 50 Pilgrims and probably about 90 Native Americans (only one Native American, Massasoit, was confirmed to be there).
3. Answers may vary, but might include wild fowl (ducks, geese, turkey) and venison (deer).
4. 1621 (sometime between September 21 or 22 and November 9)
5. Plymouth
6. Answers may vary.

Life at Plymouth (p. 17)
1. John Howland
2. Squanto
3. Smallpox and diphtheria

Compare the lifestyles of Pilgrims and Wampanoag Indians below.	Pilgrims	Wampanoag
Clothing	made of wool and linen cloth	made of animal skins
Food	bread, corn, chicken and eggs, goat milk, duck, mussels	corn, beans, squash, deer, pumpkins, cucumbers, fish
Home	houses made of bark and branches with straw for roofs	wetus with wooden poles for frames covered with woven grass mats
Education	learned respect and good manners, reading and writing from adults	learned important stories and lessons from parents and elders
Games	played marbles, ball games, board games, ran around	played ball, ran races, practiced with bow and arrow

Trivia Tracker: April 5, 1621

COLONIAL LIFE

Establishing the Colonies (p. 18)
1. F; The Quakers settled in Pennsylvania in 1682.
2. T
3. F; The colony of Jamestown was named after King James of England.
4. T
5. F; William Penn was one of the Quaker leaders.
6. T
7. T
8. F; The Puritans first settled in Massachusetts before moving to New Hampshire, Rhode Island, and Connecticut.
9. F; New Netherlands became New York in 1626.
10. T
Trivia Tracker: Roger Williams; Rhode Island

The First Permanent Colony (p. 19)
Answers may vary.

The Boston Tea Party (p. 20)
Answers may vary.

AMERICAN REVOLUTION

Revolutionary Journal (p. 21)
Answers may vary.

Battles of the Revolution (p. 22)
Battles of Lexington and Concord
When? April 19, 1775
Where? Concord and Lexington, Massachusetts
Key Figures? British General Thomas Gage; Paul Revere
Outcome? The British were forced to retreat; these battles marked the beginning of the Revolutionary War.

Battle of Bunker Hill
When? June 17, 1775
Where? Bunker Hill, Massachusetts
Key Figures? British General Thomas Gage; General Howe; Colonel William Prescott
Outcome? Americans were forced to withdraw, but British army also suffered major losses.

Battle of Saratoga
When? September 1777
Where? Saratoga, New York
Key Figures? British General John Burgoyne; American General Horatio Gates
Outcome? British surrendered on October 13, 1777

Battle of Trenton
When? Christmas, 1776
Where? Trenton, New Jersey
Key Figures? General George Washington
Outcome? The Hessians (German mercenaries fighting for the British army) were defeated.

Trivia Tracker: "Don't fire till you see the whites of their eyes."

People of the Revolution (p. 23)
Paul Revere – most famous for his "midnight ride" to Lexington, Massachusetts, to warn colonists of the British army's approach; other answers may vary
Ethan Allen – leader of Vermont's Green Mountain Boys, who fought bravely in the Revolutionary War; other answers may vary
Nathan Hale – the first American to be captured and executed by the British army for spying; other answers may vary
Deborah Sampson – disguised as a young man, she fought in the Revolutionary War for three years

A New Nation
Who Were Our Founding Fathers? (p. 24)
Answers may vary.
Trivia Tracker: 12

The Declaration of Independence (p. 25)
Answers may vary.
Trivia Tracker: 33 years old

The First President (p. 26)
Birth: February 12, 1732
Father: Augustine Washington
Wife: Martha Dandridge Custis
Number of Children: 0
Role in Revolutionary War: Commander and Chief
Political Affiliation: Federalist
Year Elected President: 1789
Vice President: John Adams
Year Left Office: 1797
Death: December 14, 1799
Trivia Tracker: Little Hunting Creek Plantation

Louisiana Purchase
The Greatest Real Estate Deal in History (p. 27)
1. France
2. Robert Livingston
3. $15 million
4. 3 cents
5. 13

What If It Had Never Happened? (p. 28)
Answers may vary.
Trivia Tracker: A French colonial prefect that turned Louisiana over to the American commissioners on December 20, 1803.

Lewis & Clark
Getting to Know Lewis & Clark (p. 29)
Answers may vary.

The Men Behind the Expedition (p. 30)
Answers may vary.

The Tale of Sacagawea (p. 31)
1. Hidatsa
2. Chief
3. Toussaint Charbonneau
4. Fur trading
5. She served as an interpreter, helped find routes and food.
6. She gave birth to her son, Jean Baptiste.
7. Chief Cameahwait, Sacagawea's brother
8. Nothing
9. William Clark adopted them.
10. Pomp or Pompey

Oregon Trail
Dear Pappy Pioneer (p. 32)
Answers may vary.

Landmarks by the Trail (p. 33)
Answers may vary.

Getting Ready to Leave (p. 34)
Answers may vary.
Trivia Tracker: $43.50

Slavery
The Life of a Slave (p. 35)
Answers may vary.

Journey to Freedom (p. 36)
Answers may vary.

The Moses of Her People (p. 37)
Birth—Born a slave in Dorchester County in Maryland around 1820 or 1826 (sources vary)
Childhood—Worked as a house servant at age 6 or 7
Teen Years—Worked in the fields. While trying to protect another slave, she got hit on the head by a heavy weight. She never fully recovered.
Adult Life—Married a free black man, but left him when she escaped from slavery. She returned to the South several times to help other slaves escape.
Trivia Tracker: $40,000

Civil War
North and South (p. 38)
Answers will vary.

Five Years of War (p. 39)
Answers will vary.
Trivia Tracker: She was a spy for the Confederacy.

Gold Rush
Golden Milestones (p. 40)
Jan. 24, 1848—James Marshall discovers gold at Sutter's Mill.
Feb. 2, 1848—Mexico signs the Treaty of Guadalupe Hidalgo, selling California to the United States.
March 9, 1848—The first gold rocker (mining tool) is used.
May 15, 1848—*The Californian*, a San Francisco newspaper, publishes a story about the discovery of gold.
Dec. 5, 1848—President Polk, in his speech to Congress, announces the discovery of gold in California.
April 1, 1849—Steamship *Oregon* arrives in San Francisco, carrying mail and passengers.
Sept. 9, 1850—California becomes the 31st state.
1854—Sacramento becomes the official capital of California.

What If? (p. 41)
Answers may vary.
Trivia Tracker: Water was scarce and many travelers were willing to pay almost anything for a cool drink of water.

WOMEN'S SUFFRAGE
Women Fighters (p. 42)
Susan B. Anthony—born 2/20/1820, died 3/13/1906; leader of women's rights movement; other answers may vary
Elizabeth Cady Stanton—born 11/12/1815, died 10/26/1902; wrote "Declaration of Sentiments"; other answers may vary
Lucretia Coffin Mott—born 1/3/1793, died 11/11/1880; called the first women's rights convention in Seneca Falls, NY, in 1848; other answers may vary
Carrie Chapman Catt—born 1/9/1859, died 3/9/1947; founded League of Women Voters; other answers may vary
Sojourner Truth—born a slave in 1797, died 11/26/1883; famous for her "Ain't I a Woman?" speech; other answers may vary
Amelia Bloomer—born 5/27/1818, died 12/30, 1894; introduced Stanton to Anthony; other answers may vary

The 19th Amendment (p. 43)
1. 1878
2. August 18, 1920
3. Parades, silent vigils, and hunger strikes
4. 36 states
5. Tennessee was the 36th state to ratify the amendment, and thus ensured the passage of the amendment.
6. The Speaker of the House and the Vice President
7. No
Children's Suffrage: Answers may vary.

THE GREAT DEPRESSION
The Lean Years (p. 44)
1. Answers may vary, but might include Germany and England.
2. Herbert Hoover
3. Unemployment rose from 1 million in 1920 to 13 million in 1933.
4. It was a term Hoover used to describe his belief that people should help themselves and not rely on the government's support.
5. Shantytowns where the unemployed were forced to live in crates and boxes

6. They collapsed as people grew afraid and withdrew all of their money.
7. Relief, recovery, and reform
8. They felt as if he had turned on his own class of people. He was a wealthy man and the wealthy could not understand why he had raised their taxes.

How Much Does It Cost? (p. 45)

Product	Price Then
	Actual
Men's Overcoat	$18.50
Men's Wool Sweater	$1.00
Suede Bag	$2.25
Women's Sweater	$1.00
Women's Bathrobe	$1.00
Women's Overcoat	$28.00
Mechanical Toys	3 for $.59
Doll	$1.95
Lamp	$1.00
Electric Washing Machine	$33.50
Gas Stove	$19.95
Wages for a Cook	$15 per week
Wages for a Doctor	$61.11 per week

WORLD WAR I
The Great War (p. 46)

	Date of First Involvement	Reason
Austria-Hungary	July 1914	Answers may vary.
Germany	August 1914	Answers may vary.
France	August 1914	Answers may vary.
Belgium	August 1914	Answers may vary.
Great Britian	August 1914	Answers may vary.
United States	April 1917	Answers may vary.
Russia	July 1914	Answers may vary.

Trivia Tracker: Manfred von Richthofen

The Causes of War (p. 47)
Imperialism—Larger European countries were ruling "smaller" countries or colonies. This led to a race between countries to gather as many colonies as possible.
Militarism—Each country wanted to have the largest military, and so started building up its own military forces to compete with those of other countries.

Nationalism—Patriotism or loyalty to one's own country; this led to wanting to have the largest military, etc.
Alliances—Two or more countries would be allied together, so that each country would be protected by the others in the alliance. If one country has an argument with another, the other countries within the alliance would be drawn in.

WORLD WAR II
Posters of Persuasion (p. 48)
Answers may vary.
Trivia Tracker: Patton was one of the most successful and controversial U.S. commanders in World War II. He was victorious in several World War II campaigns including the capture of Sicily and the invasion of North Africa.

D-Day (p. 49)
1. Rubber tanks, landing craft and false radio transmissions were located away from actual staging area.
2. Germany's main line of defense
3. Operation Overload
4. An airplane, America's first strategic bomber
5. Heavy clouds that day reduced visibility
6. 11 months
7. An amphibious truck
8. 2,500
9. 5,000
10. June 5, 1944; a storm on June 4 caused a one-day delay.
Trivia Tracker: He was the fascist dictator of Italy from 1922 to 1943. He wanted to create an empire in alliance with Hitler's Germany, but was defeated.

CIVIL RIGHTS MOVEMENT
The Woman Who Refused to Stand (p. 50)
December 1, 1955 — Rosa Parks sits down on the bus and gets arrested.
December 2, 1955 — Martin Luther King, Jr. is chosen to lead the Montgomery Bus Boycott.
December 5, 1955 — The Montgomery Bus Boycott begins.
November 13, 1956 — The Supreme Court rules that

Montgomery's segregation laws are unconstitutional.
November 14, 1956 — Rosa Parks, Martin Luther King, Jr., and E.D. Nixon board a bus. Rosa Parks sits in the front seat.
Trivia Tracker: To get off the bus and enter through a rear door

Little Rock Nine (p. 51)
Answers may vary.

King of Civil Rights (p. 52)
Answers may vary.

VIETNAM WAR
War Against Communism (p. 53)
1. 58,148
2. 19 or 22 depending on the source
3. Lyndon B. Johnson
4. Tours of duty
5. March 8, 1965
6. Richard Nixon
7. 2,200
8. 62
Trivia Tracker: 140 panels

Timeline of Events (p. 54)
Answers may vary.
Trivia Tracker: President of North Vietnam

SPACE EXPLORATION
The Right Stuff
Answers may vary.
Trivia Tracker: Johnson Space Center in Houston, Texas

Ride, Sally Ride! (p. 56)
1. May 26, 1951 in Los Angeles, CA
2. Tennis
3. Stanford
4. TFNG (Thirty-Five New Guys)
5. Date when Sally Ride became the first American woman to orbit the Earth
6. Trained to operate the robotic arm
7. Six days
8. He asked her to be on a team that investigates the January 28, 1986 *Challenger* disaster.
9. He said, "She is flying with us because she is the very best person for the job. There is no man I would rather have in her place."
10. Professor at Stanford University and University of California

What's in Store for Space? (p. 57)
Answers will vary.

AMERICAN PRIDE
Our Government (p. 58)
Amendment — a change or addition to the Constitution
Checks and Balance — the ways in which each branch of government limits the powers of the other branches of government
Constitutional — means that a law follows or is in line with the Constitution
Electoral College — the group of people who directly elect the President and Vice-President
Executive Branch — the branch of government that makes sure laws are carried out; the President is the head of this branch
Judicial Branch — the branch of government that interprets the laws
Legislative Branch — the branch of government that makes the laws
Republic — a form of government in which there is an elected president rather than a king
Trivia Tracker: A group of people who are entitled to vote

Our Flag (p. 59)

1777

1837

1863

1959

The Star-Spangled Banner (p. 60)
1. A lawyer and poet who wrote "The Star-Spangled Banner"
2. On a truce ship 8 miles from Fort McHenry
3. Key was negotiating the release of his friend, who was taken prisoner by the British army.
4. No
5. He served as a U.S. District Attorney, and also wrote several hymns for the Episcopal Church.
6. Fort McHenry
7. 1931